[where late the sweet] BIRDS SANG

[where late the sweet] BIRDS SANG

Stephen Ratcliffe

for Tom,

*know
the
form
stands*

O Books

*to
, Steve
10·27·03*

For my father

air

here

as

memory

eye

-substantial

where

to

now

in

content

waste

be—

and

———————————

or

field

very, so

small   or

being asked

sure

say

if

more

"This

excuse"—

thin

were to

see

                              face

                                        another

                    now

                    world

                                        eared

          in

      who is

                        to stop

                                    glass, an

                    A

            through

                        this

                    rememb'red

          sing

          ───────────────

                                            end

      Up

                                  nothing but

          being

                                    why

                            given

              why

                    sums yet

        traffic with

                            self

                    calls

                                        leave?

                                      with

                    to be

                              or

                         eye

              to

          which air

    -resting

                     found

                          leaves

                               where

                    distillation

          in

      effect

            remembrance what it

                                   in

                              still

    _____

                         and   face

                          still

      some

                       self-

          for

Which

      for

    ten times

Ten

               times refigured

                                   part

      ing

      not

      be

                                light

                        under

                -appearing

            looks

        having climbed the

                                middle

        or

    ending

        when

Like

        eyes ('for

                        another

                            noon

                            a son

        _____

                    ear's   music

                    not

            that which

            with

                    -tuned sounds

                end

        but

                part

        how one string

                in

    resembling

            one, one   note

                being many, seeming

                                none "

                              's eye

                         in single

               issue

        or

The world

                   form of

                private

                                      shape in mind

                          in

                place,   still

                    as

                used

                                              its

                              shame

───────────────────

        shame
        for

                                              many

                    one

             so possessed with

                                    not

                           ruin

                should

                thought, that

                air

             presence

                              - ear

                another

                    still

                          so fast

                 that

           blood

                in

                                crease

                 and

        minded so, the

                ear

                            not

           less, and

                                                more

                if

                 seal

        print more

        _____

                          that tells

                 sun

                 as

                                it

                 leaves

   Which

   And

        or

                 question

                 as

                 ties

        fast as

                            can

                            takes

you

here

Against this

other

which you

were

after

is

air

in

winter's

cold?

ear

say

———————————

star

thinks

of

ear

for

thunder, rain

say

that I in

eye

And, constant

together

store

the

end

                    everything

               but

               present   shows

        the star

           that

               ev'n by

           sap,   height

                      of memory

               constant

        most

Where

     change   /

     all in

               you

────────────────────

               not

           this

        yourself

  means

     you on the top of

                      unset

               ear your living

                  counter

           a

     pencil or

                            air

           eyes

        keep

     drawn

in

your

now

                        part

eyes

number

say, "This

touches

paper

less   than tongue

termed

meter of a

child

twice

———————

sum

and more

the

all too short

eye

                    dimmed

air

changing course

                    fade

that

                rest in

lines to

breathe

this, and

                              blunt
                    the ear
          Pluck the keen
                              -lived phoenix
                                        as

                                        if

                                        fading

                                    in

                                                    air
                    lines
                              in
                    pattern to succeed
                        or
                              in

          _____

                                                  hand painted
                                        of
                              ear, but
              shifting change
                                              less
                        whereupon it
                    hue all hues
                        eyes
                                        first
                as
                addition
          adding one thing
                                              for
                                        use

       not

           painted

           itself

                  air

     a couple

   sun and moon

           -born flow

                          hems

                    it

                 as

          though

         fixed in   air

                 say

           pose

    _____

    glass

   long as

                 furrows

                should

 or all that

       seem

                  as

     can

        be

   for myself, but

        which I will

           from

      ear

                back

                        stage

                                is part

            thing

Whose

      I   to say

                           it

                        seem to

                                love's

                     eloquence

                     speak

                        for

            tongue that

      learn to

      hear

            _____

            play

            form in

                frame

perspective

            the

                        picture

                                still

                  with

                  for eyes

            shape, and

                                    sun

                  in

      want to

      see, know

   star

                on

             whom

    Unlooked for

                                        air leaves

                          the sun's eye

                                     buried

                                  or

                 a

             thousand

       from the book

                      forgot for

                         that

             may not remove

    _____

                      to

                   my

             end this written

       witness

                                        as

                                     words to

                      some

             thought, all

                            guides

                                     air

                      tottered

       show me

                   I

       then, not show

                    as

        ear

    then begins

            in

        thoughts, from

                    to

                        open

            which

                    sight

Present

        like

                                        face

                                        mind

                        quiet

        _____

                                    light

                        of rest—

                    is not eased

        by

    each, though

                    hands

            the other

            still

        to please him

                        cloud

                        -complexioned

        sparkling stars

                            rows

            make

                                    eyes

                    cast

                                less

look

            to one

    like him, like

                                    scope

            contented

                        almost

think on the

                break of

        sings

            rememb'red

                                state

_____

                                thought

                    things past

                a

        new

            eye, unused

            in

            long since

                        vanished sight

    I

                to

                -be

        if

    I think on

restored

  all

                          supposed

                                                    loving parts

                          thought

            an

            ear

As in

      things removed

                  where

                              my

                  parts of

            many now

                        view in

                        all

      ———————————

                        content

                                          dust

                              re-

                  lines

                        'ring

                  outstripped by every

                        not

            height of

                  me but

            end's

      ear

                  in rank

            since

Theirs

                or

        mountain to

                face the

                                        alchemy

                        clouds

                                        face

        the

unseen

        sun one ear

                splendor

                                hour

                as

        this

                may stain

        _____

                        such

                travel

                                in

                                        smoke?

                        the

                        beaten face

                                a

        wound, and

                physic

                                still the

        end

                on

                pearl

                ransom

which

thorns, and silver

eclipses

test bud

in this

as

salving

more than

in sense—

part

a

war

needs

sour

———————————

two

undivided

lots

one

respect

able

though it alter

ours

know

guilt

in

name

such

port

                    take

          act

                for

          comfort

                      or

                all,   more

            parts

                  grafted to

            not

          this shadow

      in

          part

                best, that

                then

      _____

                      subject to

                breath

                a

                paper

                  thanks, if

          perusal stand

                            write to

                        invent

                  ten times

            nine

          calls on

          numbers to out

                do

          mine

man

part of

mine

but

this, let

ear

That by this

due

absence, what

sure

it

thought

teaches

here

———————————

loves

then

love, that

was

if

not

yet

wilful taste

gentle

though

now

an

ace, in

spite

that

sometime absent

it

where

to be

as

what woman's son

led?

seat for

straying

even

forced to break a two

to

me

———————————

not

it may be said

of

touches

excuse

her, be

so

for

loss

And losing

each other

is

and   are

one

wink, then

        things

    in dreams

          directed

       shadows

     shadow's form

clear

to

  say, mine

   the

      air

      sightless

       till I

        dreams

—————————————

           were thought

   distance

      space

    remote, where

        foot

       moved

           and land

As soon as think

   a

  leap

     of earth

     sure

      elements

   tear

other two, slight

both

       thought

present-absent

   these

      as

                           one

            pressed

        position

those

        now come back

          counting it

         then

        again

_____

   eye

 to divide the

           picture

               of that

         that

      pierced with crystal

          that

        air appear

     title

   of thought

by

    eye's moiety

      in

    ear

                         ear

                    now

                              for a look

                    himself

               the

          painted banquet

                                   guest

                                   a part

               picture

               present still with

                             thought

                             the

                    picture

     wakes

          _____

                                   my way

                             thrust

                    might

          hand

               to whom

               comfort, now

               rest

     left the prey

               locked up in

               not

               sure of

                                        part

                                   fear

                    prize

(if ever that

own

cast

it by

when

with that sun

in

settled gravity—

ensconce

in

this my hand

reasons

strength of

cause

_____

way

's end)

that

miles are measured

tired with

that

instinct

speed, being

not

an

answer

spurring to

put

lies onward

                              slow off

                                        speed—

                                        as

        return, of

what

                    can seem but

            spur, though

        speed

                                    keep pace

                                    being

                flesh in

                        use

                        willful

                                        to go

        _____

                                    key

                                    -locked

                                        survey

            the fine point

                                    so

                                        set

    stones

        in

            time

                        the

                    instant

                    prisoned

                        in

                                to hope

                    stance, where

millions

                        one, one

                            lend

            the counterfeit

                    you

                            set

                in

        spring and

            of

                            ear

                                now

                                    part

                                constant

    _____

how much more

            or

                    air, but air

                                in

                        as deep a

                tincture

            thorns

                                            disclose

                            how

                    respect

    the

        sweet

    so of

            shall

nor

shall

in

stone

over

the work

or

record of

all

pace

in the

ear this

judge

in this

_____

said

edge should

to

form

though

eyes

see again

perpetual

'rim like

Which parts

see

the view

being full of

more

what

times

time

do

I

watch the

absence

once

thought

or

stay and think

how

that in you

thinks

---

that

thought

at your hand

as

being

of

each check

injury

a

privilege you

belong

to pardon

it, though

sure

                              nothing

                         before

Which

                                             child!

                              a backward look

                                      sun

                         in

           mind at first

                    what

           composed

                                   where

                              the same

                              of form

           subjects

                    _____

                                                       or

                    in

                                   that which

                         forward

                              of light

                                   being

           eclipses

                                             found

                                   you

                    parallel

                         ties

      nothing

                to

      sing

image should

ear

be broken

sight?

the

home

find

scope

is

eye

that

watch

wake

near

_____

in

part

this

so grounded

thinks

a count

in

all

glass

tanned

quite

-loving

self, that

Painting

                              as
                    hand crushed
                    in

          lines
                    on
               those
                                        of

                                        spring—
          such a time
Against

                              memory
                              my
               lack
                                   still

          _____

                                        face
                         worn
          sometime
          as
               seen
                    in
               oil
                    loss, and loss
                                   of
          itself confounded
                         to
                    take
                         which cannot
                              lose

                    or stone, nor

                         way the

                              hold

                                   flower?

                         breath

                              ing

                                   out

              so

         meditation

                              chest

                                   foot back

              or

    none, unless

              ink

    _____

                    rest

    to be

              nothing

         rest

                              placed

And

And

                   limp

              tongue-

         doctor-like, control

              called

                         in

              from

         leave

should

presence

by

itself with

painting

in

directly see

of shadow, since

no

veins?

now

lives

to show what

last

————————————

of days

as

signs

inhabit

dead

right of

a second

made

hours

all

other's green

to dress

as for a map

what   was

part

nothing

tongues, the voice

              so as

           outward

those

In other accents

      farther than

look

          measure

       thought —   eyes

   add

    or match

  this

———————————

               not

        as ever

          suspect

                  air

   good, slander

    greater, being

        buds

             in

      ambush

Either

        so

     enlarged

   as

         hear

  or

                        hear

                    the world

                                                    or

                    line, remember

                                it

                in

        thinking

            say

            perhaps, compounded

                                    name

                            my

                            look

                                        gone

                    _____

            world should

                                    you

                                        forget

                        nothing

    Unless

                            mine

                                            I

                                        part

                    may

        love speak

            where my body is

                                        or

                        which

                            things

in

one, or

which

birds sang

day

after sun

a

second

glowing

a

-bed where

was

makes

leave

_____

content

all

line

still

is

part

earth, which

part

lost

my body

's knife

to be

that is

this

                        thought
            seasoned
                of
                                        found
                            anon
                    will steal
                                one
                                            pleasure
                        as in
                                look
        sing
        what is
                    in and
                    on

        _____

                    so
            from
                                            side
                            to
                still all one
                            note
    That every
                birth, and
                                    write
                    still
                    sing
                what is
                            new
                                        told

how

minutes

leave

this book

in

mouth

a

progress to

memory

blanks

in

mind

as

much

——————————

in

air as

pen

under

sing

loft

feathers to

double

that which

in

others' works

it

But

learning

one

one

numbers are decayed

place

ment

of

Yet what

pays

word

give

in

to the

not for that which

owes

———————————

write

name

a

speaking of

ocean

as

bark, in

ear

hold

sound

or

building

cast

this

                              make

                        ear

                  memory

            in

      name

      I, once gone

                              a common

                        eye

                  be

            not yet

      tongues to

            breathers of

                  —such

                  breath

      _____

                  not

                        without

                  words which

            air

                              in hue

                  a limit past

                  or

            stamp of

      so, love

            touches

            air

                              -telling

                  painting

                  blood

  need

                               no painting

        found, or thought

                          of

                             slept in

                  self

             a modern

    Speaking of

      silence

                                     being

                                     mute

                                        in

                                           air

                                              is

        _____

                                     say

                               one are you—

                                     or

                                     equal

                 in

             subject

             write

             you, so

                  what in you is

                                  made

             a counterpart

    Making

    You

    Be

  still

                        you

                    with

                        the

                            other write

                        still

                that

            form of well-

                    say

                        add something

                thought

    words come

            the breath of

                        speaking

    _____

                    of

                    to

                    in

                        where

        is spirit, by

                pitch

                    compeers

                    astonished

            that

            night

                of

        not

                                filled

                                    mine

                                        ear
           like
       charter of

                   all

                         but

               where is

                                                is

               back again

                                                      not

                         it, else

                         is on

           again, on

                   as

               waking

           _____

                                        set
                   in the eye of
                         I
       prove
           in
               part I can
           concealed

                                           much
                                     to
                                     thought
                   that
               double
                           so belong—
                         ear all

Say

    I

Speak

                            fence

                            half

    set a form upon

              knowing

              angle

            walks, and in my tongue

           name

                should

                           tell

        against myself

                  who

_____

                          if ever, now

                              to

              tune

            for an after-

                  'scaped

       ear a

          night

             over

          no

     other

  in the onset come; so

                might

                now seem

                not   so

                                        the
                                      body's
                                       angle
                              some
                                              sure

                     in
        these particulars
                              one
                    better
             than
      more
                                          men
                            alone, that
               way

        _____

                    or
        term
                    no longer than
      it
                                    ear
             the least of
             state
                                                    end
                                                    mind
                                                  lie
                         title
          to have
        what's so
                    be

                    supposing

                          —so love

        still

        looks

        there can live

                          not know

                                heart's history

        writ in moods
But
That

              thought

                    nothing

        like

                    answer

        _____

                                        one

           not

           moving

        moved, cold

                              a

                          pen

                          faces

          but

      sum

        to itself

                    as

        weed

              ing

           smell

and

Which, like a

spot

in what

tells the story

or

in a kind of

name

a

habit

every blot

can

this

edge

———————————

say

Some say

Both

faults

the finger of

be

seen

things

might

looks translate

a

strength

so

mine

                    absence

              sure of

              felt, what dark

                          where

          removed

    in

    the want

                after

          issue

                          fathered fruit

              as

                  birds

  if they sing

          look pale

          _____

                          in

          April, dressed

                  in every

      turn

          of birds

                or

              summer's

          lap

                          white

                                    rose

              figures

        you pattern

                still, and

        shadow

let thus

when

breath? The purple

for

to

hand

buds of

ear

blushing

or white, had

breath

of all

to

one could see

or color

———————

forget

which gives

song

subjects light?

or

numbers

to the ear that

both

use

If

any

everywhere

faster than

scythe

              use, what

                  of

  truth and

          too, and there

                                      say

              is color fixed

      no pencil

          best, if never

          needs

          silence so

                  gilded to

                      be

                  each

                                  show

          ————————————

                              or

          less the show

                  whose

  owner's tongue

                                  spring

                                  lays

                                  in

  stops

  that

  when

          music

                                  ear

          hold my

                              song

                              rings

                    a scope to show

                              is

                           added

                                        write

               glass

        over

               lines

                        then

               subject

        to

               you

           more, much more, than

           glass shows

        _____

                                   never can be

                                   your

                                   still. Three

               from

        Three

                    of

        April

                                   which yet are

                              like a dial

                                   no pace perceived

                                        thinks

                    in

           ear of which

                    born

                              called

                         an idol show

              like

                  one, still

                                            in

                         cell

                              confined

                    leaves out

        air

                                        words

                                     spent—

                    one, which

                                              alone

                         kept

        _____

                                   waste

                                   air

             a

        raise

        in

        hand, of foot

                    pen would

                              master

        all

                  me, all you

                                            eyes

                                       to sing

                                    present

             wonder

                           or
                    dreaming
            ease
      posed as
                                eclipse endure
                           their
         ties
                 claim
                 drops of
         looks
                                          rhyme
                          speech
                     in
                                     brass

      _____

                          ink
               figured
         to speak, what
                    love or
                            like
              say
Counting
                                     air name
                     love
                            of
                            place
                            page
                            the
                    form would show

                    say that
                absence seemed
        easy
                            which in

                        love

                            return again

                                        exchanged

                        water

                        in

                            kinds of blood

                                stained

            for
        nothing this wide

                    rose

        _____

                                        there

                        the view

                                    what

        fence

        is

        strange

                            another

        says prove

                    what

                    more will

                try

        to whom I am

            welcome, next

                    most

O for

                    of

                    or

        means which

                         name

A

        what it works in, like

                    I

                              in

                              infect

                    think

                         correction

            friend

                enough

        _____

                         impression

                stamped upon

            who calls

        -green

            the world, and

                                        tongue

                or

                sense

            found

Of others' voices

                    stopped

            my

                         purpose

                         thinks

                                    eye

                                        to go about

                                            partly blind

                seeing

                no form delivers

                                shape, which

                                                    part

                        vision

            if it see

                            favor or

                                sea, the day, or

                                shapes them

                            more, replete

                            mind

            _____

                                mind,   in

                        arch's

                        say

                                            this alchemy—

                                things

                                            resemble

        eating

                as object

                                            seeing

                                            drinks

                            knows

                    his palate

                    poisoned

                        eye

                    lines that I
                said I
                                    reason
                        after
                                        accidents
                    and change
                                        in
                        course of
        why
            not then say
            certain
            present, doubting
                    might   say
                                still

        _____

            not to
                                    not
                                    finds
        ends with
            an
            on
            to
                    unknown,   though
                                        lips
                        as
                    hours and weeks
                to the edge of
            error and
            or no

                    thus: that

                your

                    ear

                                        day by day

                                    known

                                                as

                                    wind

                transport

                                    error

                                    late

                    in the level of

            shoot not at

                        say

                                    you

            _____

                                        or

                                    palate urge—

        to

        sicken

        so, being

                                frame

                                    a kind of

                                    was

    Thus

                were

                to medicine a health

                                would

                            find

                                fell

                              of

                                 as

                              and

                                    to

                                          committed

                    thought itself

                 in

              traction

                 ill, now

                 is

                                       new

                 at first, more

                                 content

                                 than

          _____

                                    ends

              that

                       under

                 nerves were

                                       shaken

           I

     And I

                                    you

                                       rememb'red

                                          hits

           to

              salve which wound

                       as

     ransom

                    than

          to be

                lost, which

        feeling but by

                                    eyes

             or

                frailer

                    what I think good?

          am that I

             use

    may be

                thoughts

        less this

             are

          ——————————

                              in

                        memory

                            re

        date, ev'n to

                                    hear

                subsist—

                            part

        record

              could not so much

                          score

                          as

          table

      an adjunct to

              forget

not

built up

novel, nothing

a form

we

that

rather

think

registers

the present, nor

what we see

less

this

the

———————————

ear

for

subject

among weeds, or

accident

smiling

the blow

calls

here

numb

stands

it

this

who

                        bore

                   outward on

          as

Which proves more

                              form

                         too

                            simple

                            spent?

          let

       take

             mixed with seconds, know

                                   the

                         form

                         stands

          _____

                    boy, who in

                        glass

                       grown

             withering, as

                              over wrack

             onward

                    purpose, that

                                   in

                              pleasure

                 still

             delayed, answer

          quiet

                                    air

                          name

          black

                          as

                          on a

                          borrowed face

                no name, no

                not

                          eyes

            so suited, and

          who

      ring

                          becoming

              tongue

          _____

                          music

                          whose motion sounds

                fingers

                              ear

            those jacks

                      in

                      lips, which

                                          stand

                                          state

              with

              fingers walk

                                          lips

                          in this

                          lip

as

and till

full

not

one but

and

as

to

so

have

proof, and

be

now

that leads

_____

sun—

more

white, why

air

asked, red

in

some

the breath that

speak

pleasing sound

saw

walks

I think

with

as

whose

                                        ear

        air

                say

            the pow'r to make

                        bold

        ear

            that is

                but thinking on

another

        is

nothing

                        I think

_____

                and

            hear

    put on

        with

            not the morning sun

Be

        that

        half that

                        eyes

                be

        for me, since

                        part

                        self

                        complex

                that ear that

            wound it

                                    alone

                                        end

        my

        next

        myself, and

                    threefold thus to

                                            ward

                            let

                me, let my

                    use

                                        pent

                                            in me

        ——————————————

    now I

        myself am

                it, so that

                    to   still

                    not, no

                                        kind

                                to write

                            as

                                            take

                                            use

            end

        I lose

                lost

            the whole

                                    as

                          plus

                              still

              making addition

                              spacious

                    to

            others

                      air

        sea, all water, yet receives

                    add

              ing

One will

Let

Think

───────────────

                    I

                      that I

        will

              for

                              love

                                one

              of

        a

                number let

                              one

                    me, so it please the

                              thing

              my name

                              name

  to

                              what

                    is, see where it lies

                                        to

                          look

          anchored in the bay

                        as

                                              tied?

                        that

                  knows

            seeing this, say this

                              face

                                    eyes

                                        transferred

            ——————————

                        ear that

                        I know

              might think

                                                ties

                              in

                                    as

                        -speaking

              sides

          where

                    say not I

                        seem

                    not to have

                                        it

                                    be

                              on
                    lays upon my
                                                            tongue
                                        not
                                        in
                                        eye as
What
      more than
                                        well knows
                                in
                                        turns
            elsewhere might
                  so, but
                              looks

            ——————————

                                        not
            -tied
                        words, and
                        -wanting
                                        it were
                  love, yet, love, to
                                        be near
      news but
                        air I
                        might speak
            -wresting
                        ear
                        or
            eye

  eye

                              or note

                          what

                      please

                          tongue's tune

              as

          desire to be in

                                  one

                              sense

    one

              way

                      a

                                          gain

                                                  in

          _____

      is

              in, grounded on

              in

                              its

                              lips

                      scar

                  of

      others' beds

                  the

                                      tune

              that when it grows

                              be

                      what

      -example

  catch

                                                way

                            makes all

                    she

                                holds

            her who

                    flies

                    in

                that which flies

                                            behind

                        turn

                                    me, be

            that

                                    cry

        _____

                        of

    Which like two

                        man

            a woman

                                    a

                                        side

                            to

                    her

                            turn'd

    may, yet not direct

                            to each

                other's

                                but

                                    one

own hand

the sound that said, I

or

she

in

tongue

used in giving

it

an end

That followed

night, who

is

a

saying

———————————

in

that the

ear

walls

so

an

excess

charge? I

so

let that

hours

more

feed

more

                    is as
        that
Feeding on
        certain
            son, the
                                    not kept
                        now
            which physic
            reason
                        more
                            as
                                pressed
                                thought
                        dark as

        _____

        what eyes
        have
            have, where
                    what they see
                                        do
                        not so?
        not, then
                so
        it?   how
                    watching
                    I
            sees
                it
            see

                    say I

                                        take?

        think on the

                all

                    that

                                    do

                                    I not

                            present

What

That

When

                            motion

                        on, for

                        see

        ———————————

        from what

                                ear

                                                sight

                                        not

                        this becoming of

            a

            here is

        That, in

                            how to

                    hear and see

                        what others do

                                        not

                    thin

                        to

                    what

                 science is

                 not

        faults

                          a

                    body's

              body that

                                        son

      rising at

      is

      content

                 airs, fall by

        want of

           whose ear

_____

                              or

                          wearing

                          it

              after

                       each

        break twenty? I am

                    but

   all

   I have

   of

       light

                    against the

                    air: more

                    so

                              fell as

                         advantage found

                  in

            valley-

         borrowed

                     heat, still to

              see

         a

            mist

                   needs would touch

                              desired

                        temp

                     the bath

                     fire—

            _____

                                 as

                    ear

                                             to

                               hand

                       that fire

                                    warmed

            so

      Was sleeping

                           in

                  love's

         wing

               as

                     cure, and

                     water

Library of Congress Catalog Card Number: 88-062610
ISBN: 0-929022-03-3

O Books
5729 Clover Drive
Oakland, CA 94618

Distributed by:
Small Press Distribution, 1814 San Pablo Avenue, Berkeley, CA 94702
Inland Book Company Inc., 22 Hemingway Avenue, East Haven, CT 06512
Bookslinger, Inc., 502 N. Prior Avenue, St. Paul, MN 55104

Other O books:

PHANTOM ANTHEMS, Robert Grenier, 1986, $6.50
DREAMING CLOSE BY, Rick London, 1986, $5.00
ABJECTIONS: A SUITE, Rick London, 1988, $3.50
VISIBLE SHIVERS, Tom Raworth, 1987, $8.00
CATENARY ODES, Ted Pearson, 1987, $5.00
O ONE / AN ANTHOLOGY, ed. Leslie Scalapino, 1988, $10.50
A CERTAIN SLANT OF SUNLIGHT, Ted Berrigan, 1988, $9.00
RETURN OF THE WORLD, Todd Baron, 1988, $5.00
DISSUASION CROWDS THE SLOW WORKER, Lori Lubeski, 1988, $6.50